SCIENCE WITH
PLANTS

Helen Edom

Designed by Jane Felstead
Illustrated by Simone Abel

Consultant: Frances Nagy (Primary Science Adviser)

Contents

Starting to grow

Plants grow almost everywhere. This book has lots of experiments and activities to help you find out how plants live and grow.

Look around for useful things to help you grow plants, such as jars and other containers. You may need to buy some things such as flower pots and potting compost.*

Writing it down

Try keeping a nature diary to make notes and drawings about plants and your experiments. Always write the date, so you can remember when things happened and how long they took.

Looking at seeds

Plants make seeds so new plants can grow. Can you find any seeds like these in your kitchen at home?

Lentils

Rice

Dried beans

Beans are the seeds of bean plants. Look closely at a dried bean. Can you break it with your fingers?

A hard case protects the bean.

A scar shows where the bean was attached to its plant.

Soak a bean in water overnight to make it soft. Split it open carefully. What can you see inside?

Here is a tiny baby plant, ready to grow.

This part is a food store for the baby plant.

2

You can buy these at a garden center.

Growing beans

Line two jars with paper towels and add a little water. Put some dried kidney beans next to the glass, half-way up each jar. Keep them indoors.

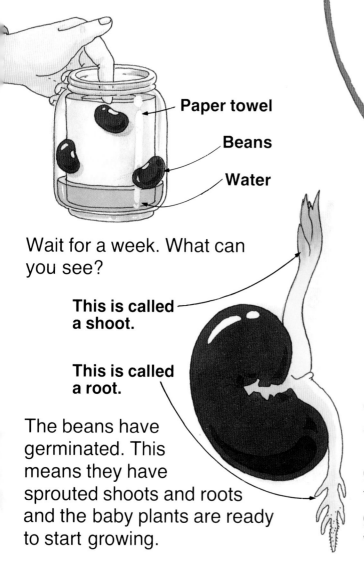

Paper towel

Beans

Water

Wait for a week. What can you see?

This is called a shoot.

This is called a root.

The beans have germinated. This means they have sprouted shoots and roots and the baby plants are ready to start growing.

Different seeds

Seeds come in different shapes and sizes. They are often inside a cover like a fruit, a shell or a pod. Here are some you might find at home.

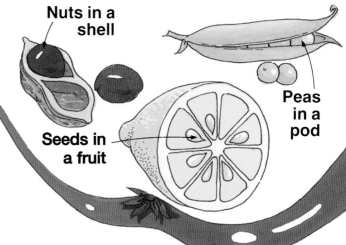

Nuts in a shell

Peas in a pod

Seeds in a fruit

Up and down

Leave one jar on its side for a few days. What happens to the way the shoots and roots grow?

Shoots always grow up towards sunlight and roots always grow down towards the ground and water.

The shoot bends up again.

The root bends down again.

3

Growing

After a seed has germinated, the young plant starts to grow. Look at the beans you germinated before (see page 3). What do you notice as they grow?

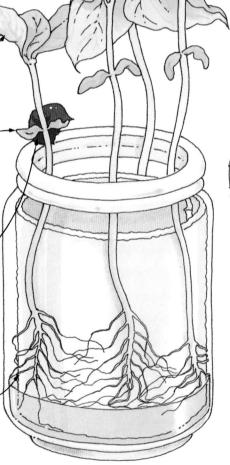

The shoots have grown leaves.

The first two leaves are very small. They are called seed leaves.

The seed cases have withered away. They are not needed anymore.

More roots have begun to grow.

How to plant beans

First fill some plastic flower pots with damp potting compost. Poke a hole in the compost with a pencil, deep enough for a seedling's roots.

Leave a dish under each pot to catch water.

Carefully take the paper towel out of the jars. Lift off the seedlings and plant one in each pot.

Push the compost down firmly around each seedling to keep it upright. Leave enough space at the top of the pot for water.

As each bean grows, its roots spread out into the compost. They take up water and hold the plant steady.

4

Healthy growing

What things do you think plants need to help them grow? Try this experiment with your potted beans to see if you are right.

Put labels on three of the pots. Put pot 1 near a window. Water it every three days.

Put pot 2 near a window but do not water it.

Put pot 3 in a dark cupboard. Water it every three days.

After three weeks see which plant has grown best.

Pot 1 should grow best because it has soil, light and water. Plants need all these things to stay healthy.

Speedy grower

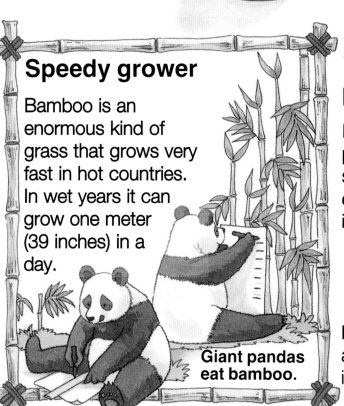

Bamboo is an enormous kind of grass that grows very fast in hot countries. In wet years it can grow one meter (39 inches) in a day.

Giant pandas eat bamboo.

How fast?

How fast do your bean plants grow? Hold some cardboard beside each one and measure its height each day.

You can tie a tall plant to a stick to keep it straight.

How high is each plant after a month? Keep notes in your nature diary.

Plants and water

Water gets into a plant from the ground through the roots. What do you think happens to it next?

Climbing up the stem

Put a stick of celery into a jar of water. Add a few drops of blue ink.

Leave the jar near a window for four hours. What happens to the leaves?

The leaves are full of blue inky water. Plants suck water up through the stem into the leaves. They need water to grow and keep healthy.

Water getting out

Cover a potted plant with a clear plastic bag, and tie it around the stem. Stand it in a sunny place. Look at the bag after four hours and rub it with your fingers.

Can you see tiny water droplets?

Plants do not use all the water they take up. They get rid of extra water through tiny holes in their leaves. The bag traps the droplets so you can see them.

Cut a slice from the stem. What can you see?

Tiny blue dots show the tubes that carry water up the stem.

*Never put plastic bags near your face or mouth.

6

Make a bottle garden

You can make a garden that never needs watering. Find a large bottle or jar with a lid. Lay it on its side and fill it with layers like this.

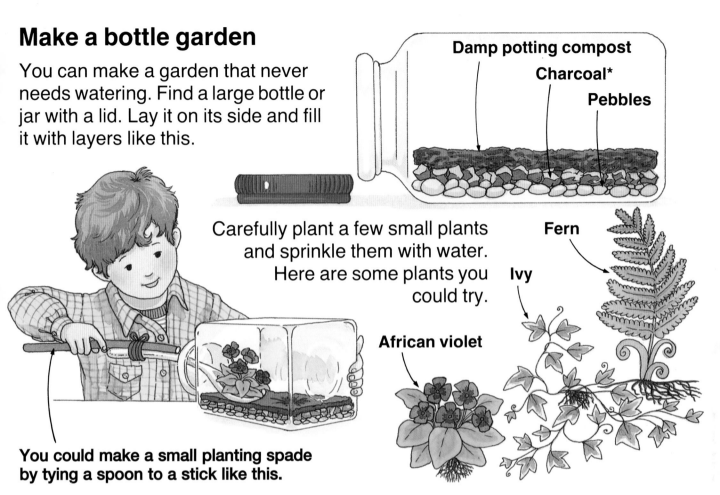

Damp potting compost
Charcoal*
Pebbles

Carefully plant a few small plants and sprinkle them with water. Here are some plants you could try.

Fern
Ivy
African violet

You could make a small planting spade by tying a spoon to a stick like this.

Put the lid on the bottle and leave it in a warm, light place. The plants should keep on growing healthily.

The plants get water through their roots and lose it through their leaves. It is trapped inside the bottle and trickles down so the plants can use it again and again.

You can get this from a garden center. 7

Using light

Plants need light to live. These experiments will help you to find out why.

Looking for light

Leave a potted plant in a room with one window. Put it a little way from the window and water it as usual.

What do you notice about the way the plant grows?

Which side do the leaves grow on?

The plant leans towards the light. If you turn the pot around, the plant soon grows back to face the window again. Plants always grow towards light.

In the dark

Cover one leaf of a growing plant with foil so that it gets no light.

Take the foil off after a week. What do you notice?

Without light the leaf turns yellow. The other leaves are still green.

Making food

Plants use energy from sunlight to make food. Leaves have special green stuff called chlorophyll, that traps the sun's energy. Without light, leaves cannot make food. They turn yellow and the plant dies.

Looking at leaves

What things do you notice when you look at a leaf?

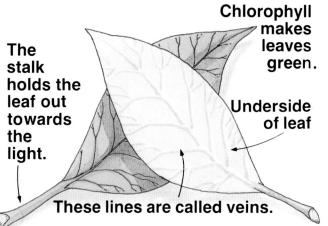

Chlorophyll makes leaves green.

The stalk holds the leaf out towards the light.

Underside of leaf

These lines are called veins.

Can you feel veins with your fingers? Water moves along them to all parts of a leaf. Veins also take food from the leaf to the rest of the plant.

Leaf shapes

Have you noticed how the leaves on a plant are usually the same shape?

Every plant has different leaves. A leaf's shape can tell you which kind of plant it comes from.

Leaf prints

Collect as many different kinds of leaves as you can.

Put the leaves on some cardboard, and lay a piece of paper over them.

Rub over the paper with a wax crayon or soft pencil to make the shape of the leaf appear.

Always rub in the same direction.

Try using different colors.

Label each leaf so that you know which plant it comes from.

Flowers

Flowers are the parts of plants that make seeds. They come in many shapes, sizes and colors.

Look at a rose. It has the same main parts as most flowers.

These colored parts are called petals.

These green parts are sepals.

You can see sepals on the outside of a flower bud. They protect the petals until the petals grow big enough to push the sepals open.

Carefully pull the petals off the rose. How many are there? What shape are they? Can you smell them?

Petals have bright colors and sweet smells to attract insects to the plant.

Shapes and colors

Each kind of flower has different petals, with their own shape, color and smell. Here are some you might know.

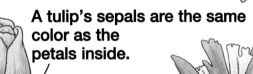

A daffodil's petals are joined together to make a trumpet.

A tulip's sepals are the same color as the petals inside.

An iris's petals have different colors and shapes.

Making seeds

What can you see inside a rose?

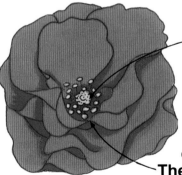

This group of yellow parts right in the middle is called a pistil.

These are called stamens. They grow around the pistil.

The stamens and pistil make seeds for new plants.

10

Powder

Look at the stamens through a magnifying glass. Gently touch the tips.

Can you find any yellow powder? This is called pollen. It brushes off the stamens easily.

Sometimes pollen from one flower reaches the pistils of another of the same kind. Then the plant starts to make seeds. This is called pollination.

Smelly flower

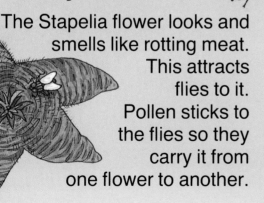

The Stapelia flower looks and smells like rotting meat. This attracts flies to it. Pollen sticks to the flies so they carry it from one flower to another.

Helpful insects

Look for insects on flowers outside during summer. How many kinds can you see?

Insects come to drink a sweet juice made inside a flower. This is called nectar.

Watch a butterfly on a flower. You can see it drinking nectar with its long tongue.

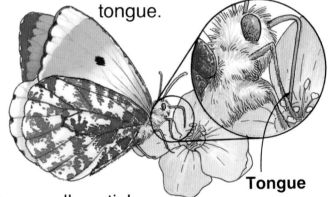

Tongue

Some pollen sticks to insects. They carry it from one flower to another. This is how most flowers are pollinated.

Lots of pollen sticks to a bee's furry body.

Trees

Trees can grow bigger than any other plants. Look at trees near your home. How tall are they? Are any taller than a house?

Oldest of all

A bristlecone pine tree growing in California in the USA, is over 4,600 years old. It is the oldest living tree on Earth.

Growing old

Look at the top of a tree stump. What can you see?
There are lots of rings in the wood. Trees make one ring every year. So the number of rings tells you how old the tree is.

The middle rings are the oldest.

This ring was made two years ago.

Stealing the light

Stand under a big tree in summer and look up.*
Can you see the sky?

The leaves make food for the tree.

A big tree needs to make lots of food, so it has many leaves. They spread out to catch as much light as possible. This is why you can't see much sky.

Ask an adult before you go out on your own.

Living in trees

Look closely at a big tree near your home and watch it every day. How many living things can you see or find in it?

Caterpillars eat leaves.

Squirrels eat nuts, seeds and shoots.

Birds like woodpeckers nest in holes in the trunk.

Some plants such as ivy grow on trees.

Fungi grow on the tree trunk.

Watching trees
In your nature diary you can write down everything you notice about trees and what lives in them. Don't forget to write the date above each entry.

Dropping off

Watch trees through the year. What happens to their leaves?

In fall the leaves of many trees turn yellow and fall off. Soon the trees are bare.

The leaves drop off because it gets too cold for trees to make food. They stop growing all winter.

New leaves

When it warms up in spring, new leaves appear and start to make food. Now the tree can grow again.

Some trees such as holly keep their leaves all year. They are called evergreens.

13

New plants from old

In winter some plants lose their leaves and other plants disappear beneath the ground. But this does not mean they are dead. They are taking a rest from growing. In the spring they start again.

Ready for spring

Take a walk in winter when there are no leaves on the trees. Pick a few twigs from different trees and look at the ends. What can you see?

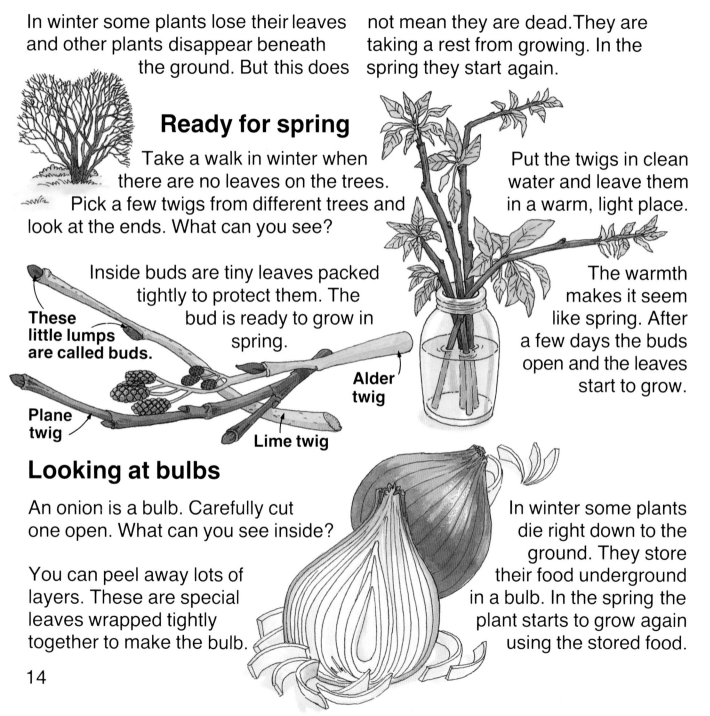

Inside buds are tiny leaves packed tightly to protect them. The bud is ready to grow in spring.

These little lumps are called buds.

Plane twig

Lime twig

Alder twig

Put the twigs in clean water and leave them in a warm, light place.

The warmth makes it seem like spring. After a few days the buds open and the leaves start to grow.

Looking at bulbs

An onion is a bulb. Carefully cut one open. What can you see inside?

You can peel away lots of layers. These are special leaves wrapped tightly together to make the bulb.

In winter some plants die right down to the ground. They store their food underground in a bulb. In the spring the plant starts to grow again using the stored food.

14

Growing bulbs

You can grow an Amaryllis bulb in a jar with a narrow neck. Fill the jar with water and balance the bulb on top so that it just touches the water. Leave the jar in a warm, dark place.

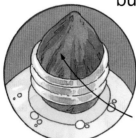

Bulb

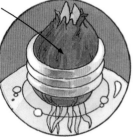

After a few days the bulb grows roots and shoots. Now you can put it in the light.

After a while a flower begins to grow.

A bulb does not need soil. It has everything inside it for a plant to start growing again.

The roots grow down to the bottom of the jar.

Growing carrot tops

You can grow plants from kitchen scraps such as carrot tops. A carrot stores food ready for a plant to grow again, just like a bulb does.

Put a carrot top in a saucer of water and leave it in a warm, bright place. What do you see after two or three weeks?

Don't let the water dry up.

The carrot top sprouts leaves.

Beet leaves

Try growing other kitchen scraps. Uncooked beet tops grow big, colorful leaves.

Plants leaving home

If plants grow crowded together, they do not get enough light, soil or water. Plants have lots of different ways to help their seeds spread out into new places.

Clinging on

After your walk look closely at your clothes. Sometimes you can find little round things called burrs stuck there. These have seeds inside.

Getting a lift

After a walk outdoors, carefully scrape the mud off your shoes.*

Put the mud into a wet plastic bag.

Close it and leave it in a warm place. What happens after a week or so?

Can you see shoots starting to grow? Plants have germinated from tiny seeds in the mud. You have helped to spread the plants by carrying their seeds on your shoes.

Look at one burr closely under a magnifying glass. What can you see?

Burr   **Tiny hooks**

Burrs have tiny hooks that cling to things like animals' fur or your clothes. In this way the seeds inside are carried away to grow in new places.

Burrs come from plants like this.

Burrs stick to fur.

*Always wear rubber or gardening gloves when handling soil.

Blowing in the wind

Pick the head off a dandelion after the flower has died. What happens when you blow it?

Dandelion seeds are carried by lots of tiny, fluffy parachutes.

The parachutes are so light that the wind can carry them away. How far can you blow them?

Many plants use the wind to scatter their seeds. Look at the seeds of sycamore or maple trees. They are shaped like wings. What happens if you hold one up high and drop it?

The seeds spin like tiny helicopters.

This makes them fall slowly, so breezes have time to blow them away from the tree.

Ask a friend to drop some sycamore seeds. Fan them with a magazine as they fall. How far do they blow?

Can you find any other seeds that travel by wind? Which ones can you blow the furthest?

> Ash seed
>
> Elm seed

Looking tasty

Many plants have bright-colored berries. In winter, berries are eaten by birds like thrushes. They scatter the seeds in their droppings, so the plants are spread to new areas.

Plants and soil

Most plants grow in soil. Their roots spread out to keep the plant steady and to find water. These experiments will help you find out more about soil.

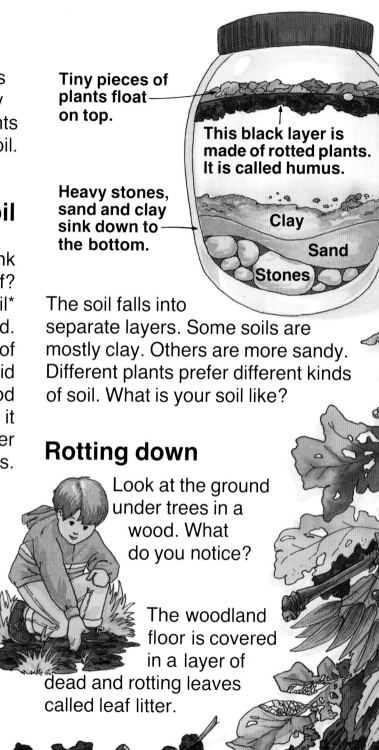

Tiny pieces of plants float on top.

This black layer is made of rotted plants. It is called humus.

Heavy stones, sand and clay sink down to the bottom.

Clay

Sand

Stones

Inside soil

What do you think soil is made of? Put a scoop of soil* into a jar with a lid. Add two scoops of water. Put on the lid and give it a good shake. Shake it up again after two hours.

You could use a yogurt pot as a scoop.

The soil falls into separate layers. Some soils are mostly clay. Others are more sandy. Different plants prefer different kinds of soil. What is your soil like?

Rotting down

Look at the ground under trees in a wood. What do you notice?

The woodland floor is covered in a layer of dead and rotting leaves called leaf litter.

Let the jar stand. What can you see one day later?

Close up

Collect some leaf litter in a plastic bag. Shake it out onto paper at home and search through it carefully to see what you can find.*

Crawling with life

Look more closely at your leaf litter. Can you spot any animals like these?

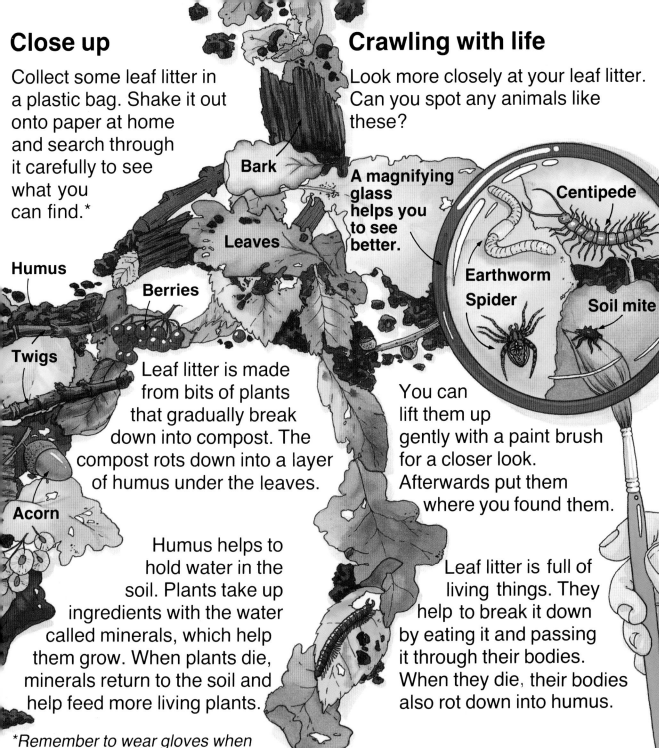

Bark

Leaves

Humus

Berries

Twigs

Acorn

A magnifying glass helps you to see better.

Centipede

Earthworm

Spider

Soil mite

Leaf litter is made from bits of plants that gradually break down into compost. The compost rots down into a layer of humus under the leaves.

You can lift them up gently with a paint brush for a closer look. Afterwards put them where you found them.

Humus helps to hold water in the soil. Plants take up ingredients with the water called minerals, which help them grow. When plants die, minerals return to the soil and help feed more living plants.

Leaf litter is full of living things. They help to break it down by eating it and passing it through their bodies. When they die, their bodies also rot down into humus.

Remember to wear gloves when handling soil.

Useful plants

People use plants in lots of ways. How many things in your home do you think come from plants?

Lots of different parts of plants can be eaten. You can probably find some in your kitchen.

Flour is made from crushed wheat seeds. Bread, spaghetti and many other things are made with flour.

Many of the things you use every day are made from parts of plants.

Most paper is made from wood that is crushed and pulped.

Some soap is made from oils that are squeezed out of plants.

Walnuts are seeds.

Bananas are fruit.

Celery sticks are stalks.

Cabbages are leaves.

Onions are bulbs.

Wooden furniture is made from trees.

Cotton is woven from the fluffy outside of cotton seeds.

This shows a cotton seed.

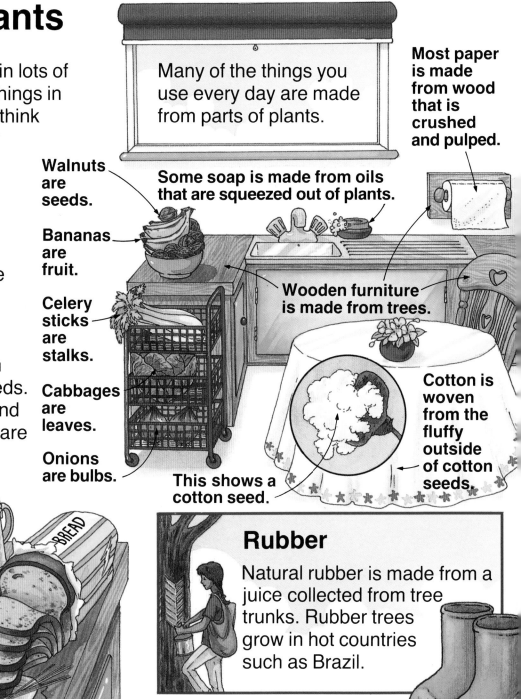

Rubber

Natural rubber is made from a juice collected from tree trunks. Rubber trees grow in hot countries such as Brazil.

Plants in danger

Pollution is waste and rubbish left by people that harms living things. Traffic fumes are a kind of pollution. Here you can see how they damage plants.

On a dry day, gather some leaves growing near a road in a town.*

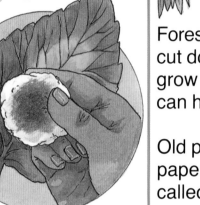

Wipe them with a damp tissue. Can you find any dirt?

Some of this dirt comes from traffic fumes. It blocks out the light that leaves need to make food.

Try wiping leaves picked in a park or garden. They should be much cleaner.

*Always be very careful near roads. Ask an adult to go with you.

Protecting trees

Forests in many places are being cut down faster than they can grow back. Here is one way you can help to protect trees.

Old paper can be made into new paper and used again. This is called recycling. It means fewer trees need to be cut down to make paper.

You could collect old newspapers for recycling. Ask a grown up where to take them.

Try to buy only recycled paper if you can. Use old envelopes again.

Notes for parents and teachers

These notes are intended to help answer questions that might arise from the activities on earlier pages.

Growing (pages 4–5)

At first the plant without light (pot 3) will grow fastest. This is because light prevents excessive growth. However, without light the plant cannot make food. Its leaves turn yellow and it soon dies.

Plants and water (pages 6–7)

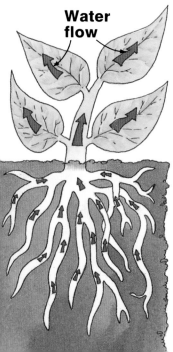

Water flow

Water travels to all parts of a plant through tubes called xylem vessels. It is lost from holes in the leaves called stomata and evaporates. This helps to pull more water up through the plant. The flow of water through a plant is called transpiration.

Light and food (pages 8–9)

Plants use light to make food in their leaves by a process called photosynthesis. Leaves contain a green substance called chlorophyll which absorbs energy from sunlight. Carbon dioxide from the air enters the leaves through the stomata and water reaches them from the roots.

Sunlight

Carbon dioxide

Chlorophyll in leaves

Food

Water

The chlorophyll uses the trapped energy in a chemical reaction to combine the water and carbon dioxide. This makes glucose (a kind of sugar). Tubes in the stem called phloem vessels carry this food to all parts of the plant.

Flowers (pages 10–11)

Flowers contain a plant's sex organs. The stamens are male and the pistil is female. At the bottom of the pistil are

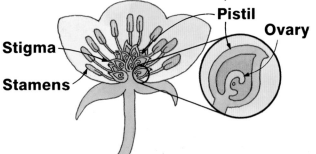

Stigma

Stamens

Pistil

Ovary

ovaries with eggs inside. In some plants, such as red campion, the male and female organs are within separate flowers on separate plants.

Flowers cannot move so they rely on either insects or wind to transfer pollen grains from the stamens to a stigma – the sticky tip of a pistil. When a pollen grain lands on a stigma, it grows a tube down to the ovary at the bottom of the pistil. Tiny male sex cells travel down the tube to fertilize the egg.

Trees (pages 12–13)

Trees grow a new layer of wood every year. The growth takes place in an area called the cambium which is between the wood and the bark. As the tree gets older, old cells in the middle die and form a tough wood called the heartwood.

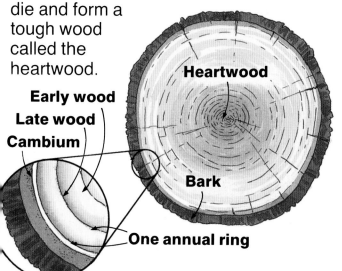

Early wood
Late wood
Cambium

Heartwood

Bark

One annual ring

New plants from old (pages 14–15)

After flowering, the bulb's food supply is exhausted. You can only grow a new flower from the same bulb next year if you plant it, so it can get nutrients from the soil.

Soil (pages 18–19)

Compost is partially decomposed matter that has not yet rotted right down to humus. Humus is dead organic matter which has rotted down and lost all its shape. It forms a sticky coating around soil particles that absorbs water and holds it for plants to take in. Nutrients and mineral salts dissolve into the water and are also taken up by the plants.

Useful plants (pages 20–21)

In addition to the paper industry, trees are felled for fuel, timber and to provide space for farmland. Forests, especially tropical rainforests, are very important to the world's climate. They maintain the balance of oxygen and carbon dioxide and release water into the atmosphere. Over half the world's rainforests have already been destroyed.

Index

First published in 1992 by Usborne Publishing Ltd., Usborne House, 83-85 Saffron Hill, London, EC1N 8RT, England. www.usborne.com Copyright© 2006, 1992 Usborne Publishing Ltd.

The name Usborne and the devices ♀ 🎈 are trade marks of Usborne Publishing Ltd.
Printed in China. AE.